EXCUSES,
EXCUSES

You don't want to get your new shorts wet? Do you suppose David Hasselhof worries about getting his shorts wet?
Gray

GRAY JOLLIFFE & LESLEY-ANN JONES

EXCUSES, EXCUSES

HOW TO DUCK, WEAVE AND WRIGGLE OUT OF ANY SITUATION

KYLE CATHIE LIMITED

First published in Great Britain in 1996 by
Kyle Cathie Limited
20 Vauxhall Bridge Road
London SW1V 2SA

ISBN 1 85626 182 4

Illustrations copyright © 1996 by Gray Jolliffe
Text copyright © 1996 by Lesley-Ann Jones

Gray Jolliffe and Lesley-Ann Jones are hereby identified as the
illustrator and author of this work in accordance with Section 77 of
the Copyright, Designs and Patents Act 1988.

A Cataloguing in Publication record for this book is available from
the British Library.

Edited by Caroline Taggart
Designed by the Senate

Printed in Spain by Cayfosa Industria Gráfica

Not that I care, but where is your husband?

Why, he's dead.

I'll bet he's just using that as an excuse.

I was with him till the very end.

Huh! No wonder he passed away.

I held him in my arms and kissed him.

Oh, I see. So it was murder.

GROUCHO MARX AND MARGARET DUMONT IN *DUCK SOUP*

My inability to stay awake is congenital. It's right there in my DNA—I can't fight it.

CONTENTS

A POOR EXCUSE FOR AN INTRODUCTION

When all is said and done, money, sex and excuses are what make the world go round. so we all know where we stand, don't we?

But there's a catch. It's a sad and baffling fact that, while you can usually beg, borrow or steal money in a crisis - even exchanging it for sex in a real emergency - the perfect excuse is often excruciatingly elusive. It is the one thing that you really would give your right arm for in those all too frequent moments when you dig yourself deeper and deeper into the blackest hole from which it seems you may never emerge.

For example.

Both your ex-wives, one of whom you left for the other, have expressed the wish to stay with you in your London home at the same time as your mother, who unfortunately despises them both. One of your ex-wives is a former *Vogue* model and accused you at the time of the divorce of only having married her for her looks. You don't want to prove her right, so you are not sure where you are going to hide the current 19-year-old blonde Scandinavian. Worse, a favourite painting of the other ex-wife, worth ten grand, which she graciously decreed at the time of the divorce should be left hanging over the fireplace, has been flogged to pay the mortgage. You are well behind on both alimony payments, but have just purchased a brand new Ferrari Testarossa, which now sits immobilised with a battery problem right in front of the house. What on earth do you do?

You read this book - that's what you do, preferably before everyone arrives

On the other hand, if you feel you could use a little help in the 'Letting Someone Down Gently' department, fear not: I have sometimes found that the literary equivalent of blinding a person with science will do the trick. Always keep a few quotes along the lines of this one from Cervantes up your sleeve:

'Ah, madame, I would give an empire to purchase your desirable charms, but fortune, that unrelenting enemy of the truly deserving, has harried me, and riveted me to my work.'

Has a more palatable ring to it than 'Sorry love, got to work late at the office', wouldn't you agree?

If you would – let's talk. And if, by the end of this manual, you are not wriggling, ducking and weaving your way out of any given crisis like a good'un, then we might be able to discuss some sort of a refund. Only trouble is, what with publishers' percentages, the rate of inflation and the demise of the net book agreement, not to mention the tardy alimony payments, you may be better off hawking this to your nearest car boot sale. One word of advice: should you opt for the latter, don't take the Ferrari, and adopt a credible disguise just in case the second ex-wife drops by in time to see you flogging the fur coat she left behind after her last visit.

THE ANATOMY OF THE EXCUSE

EXCUSES – WHO NEEDS 'EM?

It cannot have escaped your notice that there are times in our gentle waltz through life when there comes a sudden searing, screeching noise from the first violin section. The music stops and there you stand, caught painfully in the glaring spotlight of life. The cry has gone up, 'What's your excuse this time, then ?' You feel completely alone, shocked – naked even (perhaps you are – see page 156).

The question demands a reply. You play back the truth in your head, and it sounds completely feeble. Circumstances have once again backed you into a corner, and there is nothing for it but to reach for that crucial survival tool, the plausible excuse. You begin to invent. And once you are halfway down that steep and slippery slope, you might just as well make the most of it.

Let's face it, it's not your fault.

OUT OF THE MOUTHS OF BABES. . .

All too few of us are born with a silver excuse in our mouth. The best most of us can manage in our early years as a playground renegade is 'It wasn't me, Miss' (pointing shiftily at any less clued-up classmate who looks as if they might carry the can). More subtle techniques must be sought if you are to survive in adult life and these are acquired only through experimentation and commitment.

Myself, I blame the parents. They send us off out into the world armed with a concept which, though laudable in principle, has its limitations in practice. I'm talking about the idea that 'honesty is the best policy'. It is drummed into you from birth and, as you grow up, the sound of this drum grows increasingly hollow and distant.

However, like the dutiful progeny you are, you venture forth with the praiseworthy intention of clinging to the Staff of Truth. And you do, on many an excruciating occasion, and barely live to tell the tale. You learn to your cost that when somebody asks you how you are, they don't really want to know. You discover the hard way that when Aunt June enquires sweetly what you think of her darling daughter's nuptial get-up on the big day, she seeks only your gushing approbation, not the warts-and-all low-down on why chunky girls with billiard-table legs should show nothing below the knee.

At work, it is the same story. You find that your long-suffering boss doesn't want to hear that you were late for work yet again because there really was a derailment, fatality, leaves on the line or a falling of the wrong kind of snow.

Indeed, it is often the case that the truth does absolutely nothing to enhance your office status or chances of promotion; to stagger back from a liquid lunch drunk as a fiddler's bitch and to admit gaily to your head of department that you are drunk as a fiddler's bitch achieves very little in the grand scheme of things. To take matters further by regurgitating the chicken and mayonnaise sandwich you have just hastily consumed in the lift into the waste-paper bin beside her desk is tantamount to professional suicide, even if it does add weighty evidence to the truth.

On other occasions, excuses may conceal the noblest of motives. Indeed, the world of the excuse is a deep, subtle and ultimately caring place. It's not all about avoidance and subterfuge (although these bits are the most fun) and there's a lot to be said for employing a verbal ruse in order to spare someone's feelings. In spurning an advance, for example, you don't want to be deliberately hurtful (nor to be remembered for your nastiness/trembling frigidity), but you do want to get your message across. There are ways of doing this. More on this later.

There are times, of course, when even you have to admit that you are just plain wrong. You've bungled. You've been caught with a paw in the cookie jar of life, and you have some serious explaining to do. At such times, it is important to 'be prepared' in the true Baden-Powell sense of the phrase; to know in advance how to cope with such a situation. Hence the need to master the art of the excuse.

EXCUSES IN THE DOCK

'So, to sum up the case for the defence, Your Honour, we have heard that unconsidered honesty is not all it's cracked up to be. That life's a bitch (beggin' your pardon). That the slings and arrows of outrageous fortune often back us into corners from which we have no obvious means of escape and that while the "Whole Truth and Nothing But The Truth" is all very well in its way, more often than not it is simply not enough. The post-recession '90s are hard times, and nowadays it's about every man for himself, and doing and saying whatever it takes just to get by. In other words, if you can get out of something tricky while saving someone else's feelings, or stop beating yourself up over perceived personal failure by acquiring a more positive attitude, and generally grease, charm and disarm your way through life without ever being found out, then why do things the hard way?'

I rest my case.

Thus is the excuse rendered totally and utterly excusable.

OTHER PEOPLE

Excuses, just like those who deploy them, come in all shapes and sizes. The most obvious, and perhaps broadest category with the most scope for glorious technicolor no-holds-barred invention, comprises those excuses you make to Other People.

Now Other People are all well and good in themselves. Indeed, some of my best friends are Other People. But the fact is that they have the annoying habit of stealing a march on you, or of momentarily holding the balance of power – just when you thought you had your own sticky mitts on the damn thing.

Call me paranoid if you must (I am being watched, you know), but these Other People are the enemy. Get to know them. Study their every move. Buy some expensive books on body language. Better still, buy another copy of this book – you can't be over-prepared and if you bought enough, you could always hide behind a stack of them in a real crisis. In fact, if you hear the accusation 'Excuses, excuses' you're probably too late anyway. You have to hear it coming, develop a sixth sense, and cut the enemy off at the pass. If Hollywood can have a prequel, why can't we have a pre-emptive excuse, a sort of 'pre-cuse'?

A few tips here – at no extra cost. Look for danger signals. Be ready with the get-out clause. Always expect the worst (let's face it, that's what's going to happen) and arm yourself accordingly. Being prepared doesn't (necessarily) mean carrying a packet of condoms in your handbag. We are talking pre-planning, execution of plan, delivery and follow-up.

Finally, try considering excuses as objects of rare beauty. At their very best they become sublimely undetectable. However, they are almost as delicious if they place the user beyond reasonable contradiction. No one likes a scene – not even Other People.

EXCUSES TO OURSELVES

There's a fair chance that you would have been reading this a good nine months ago, had I managed to get around to finishing it. Fact is, what with moving house, finding new schools for the kids, getting the ads out for a new cleaning lady/gardener/odd-job man/babysitter, the spell of depression I knew I was heading for brought on by the stress of moving, the week I had to take at that health farm in Berkshire with my sister to get over the shock of discovering that my husband wasn't having an affair, the fortnight's holiday we had to arrange at the last minute in order to bond again as a family, the general disarray of house, home and garden, not to mention the anxiety over missing shoes, mouldy fridge and starving budgie on our return, I just haven't had a nanosecond to myself. You know how it is. . .

Such are the sad excuses we make for ourselves. A tricky area, this, because, although we can make excuses to others and, having done the necessary, breathe a hefty sigh of relief at a job well done as we pour ourselves a celebratory quadruple vodka, there is no escaping our conscience, the nagging inner voice. Okay, voices. Call me a nutter, but I can't possibly be the only one who hears several. Anyway, you know the kind of thing: 'It's not my fault that I spend all day in the pub/in front of the telly/ in the bath/ in bed underneath the nanny, instead of getting on with my work.' 'There's no point going on a diet, the mere thought of it makes me eat more.' 'Of course it's okay to sleep with more than one woman at a time – as long as they don't all work in the same building/live in the same flat/I remember to call them by the right names. And anyway, the great sex we're having is probably the only thing saving their marriages.'

You may be well aware that you have had to fall back regularly on a variety of fairly harmless excuses in order to justify your lifestyle to yourself. You may, however, until this very moment, have been oblivious to the fact that you are in the habit of lying to yourself. I know I am.

"Look, have you come here to confess or just to make a string of excuses?"

By way of an excuse, it is worth remembering here that life is hard enough without cutting a rod with which to beat yourself (leave that to those who love you) and that there is not enough room in the house for another saint.

The great thing about self-deluding excuses is that if they are used often enough they take on the form of reality. This is not quite as pathetic as lying to all and sundry and coming to believe your own lies – we've all had a boss like that. But why live in the real world when a rose-tinted parallel universe, a place where you can write your own script, is yours for the taking?

PRACTICE MAKES PERFECT

Corny, but true. Although the weight of wisdom contained in this book will surely give the binders a headache, it cannot do it all for you. You have to go out into the world and experiment, test yourself and see how well you fare.

Why not try getting yourself into trouble just to see how skilful you are at extricating yourself ? Better still, try getting someone else into trouble, and see if you can learn anything from them.

Once you have got your head around the necessity and viability of making excuses, you can use this manual in the privacy of your own home, without fear of arrest, to help you compare and contrast the various types of excuses. Try running little scenarios in your head – play the megalomaniac. You'll know when you've really got the hang of it, because the happy endings will start to outnumber those in which you have sizeable portions of egg all over your face.

A word of caution here – while you are hunched in rapt concentration over this book, remember not to mumble too much – Other People are bound to suspect something. This, after all, is not a matter you can talk through with even your closest friend or family member, as these are the very people upon whom you will be needing to practise your art from time to time. Wrap the book in brown paper, carry it about in a supermarket carrier bag or read it under the duvet by torchlight in the dead of night.

It's also worth keeping in mind that if you have to lie, a woppa's a woppa, whatever the size. Don't stint yourself. As they say, there's no such thing as being a bit pregnant.

TYPES AND TECHNIQUE

It is important to recognise the difference between those excuses which have to be deployed as one-offs and those which can be used time and time again to ever-increasing effect. Likewise, you will occasionally come across the politically incorrect excuse: it is a sad and inexcusably sexist fact that some excuses remain the distinct domain of women and others of men. Here are some techniques you should develop and learn how to apply:

* avoidance
* denial
* exaggeration
* passing the buck

* creating a diversion
* hiding
* grovelling
* having an alibi
* keeping one eye on the exit
* conjuring
* fainting
* use of props
* use of pager / mobile phone
* enlisting the assistance of an accomplice (a tricky one this, you never know who you can trust)
* pretending to be foreign
* bare-faced lying

and, as a last resort,

* insanity

THINK BEFORE YOU DUCK, WEAVE OR WRIGGLE

Important point, this. Don't be too quick or eager to advance an excuse until you have assessed precisely how the land lies. You may not need one. Sure, at the first sign of a crisis, that tell-tale whiff of smoke, the inclination to jump right in there and slap one on the table is instinctive. The eyes glaze over, the jaw drops and the tongue is thrown into top gear well before the brain is engaged. This is quite understandable when the voice of paranoia is screaming in your ear, 'Do something! Say something! Anything! Quick!' But you will learn to control this urge. It is merely that without realising it you have leaned on your internal panic button. The best thing to do is buy some time – a fixed enigmatic grin and distant stare works for me (but people are starting to talk).

KEEP A CLEAR HEAD

Are you sitting comfortably? You are going to have to give up drinking. Now. For good. Or at least until you get the hang of all this and are quietly confident that you can function excusefully with a less than clear head.

Why do you think Californians don't drink? It's because, as a Hollywood movie executive once said to me, 'They have to remember the lies they tell.' I assume he included himself in the category – he drank only Palm Spring at lunch and spent the sunny afternoons lying through his back teeth to an astonishing line-up of personnel, including his shrink, his pool operative, his manicurist, his nutritionist, his dogs, and, quite possibly at the end of the day, himself. I can't help thinking that there must have been something else in that mineral water.

At this point the balanced, rational excuser will raise one eyebrow and say, 'Hell, look at the Californians, what a screwed-up mess! Waiter, fetch me another pomegranate daiquiri . . .'

CASE HISTORIES

There now follow a few examples of putting your hard-learned excuses into practice. Either by yourself, or with the help of a series of life-like cardboard cut-outs, imagine yourself in each of these typical situations and act out the role of the excuser until you feel super-confident. Then work up the courage to try them out for real. Be warned, however: there are certain aspects of each area which may be best avoided until or unless you really find yourself caught in the dire emergency in question. In which case, you have nothing to lose. So tally ho, old bean, no holds barred, feel free, sleeves up, party on down and go for it!

CASE NUMBER ❶: IT'S NOT WHAT IT SEEMS/WAIT, I CAN EXPLAIN...

You are at a party, and the once-in-a-lifetime opportunity presents itself to bury yourself among the curves of luscious, long-legged Lizzie from Liverpool (or Los Angeles or Lima or Launceston – we excusers are citizens of the world). There you are, a grateful palm beneath each heavenly orb, your disbelieving nose wedged neatly into her scented, faintly freckled cleavage, when in walks your wife. . .

Do you leap like a startled buck and dive through the nearest window (open or closed)? No, you do not! Instead, upon hearing the strangled vowels of She Who Must Be Obeyed (and quite possibly the crack of the bull-whip she keeps in her bag), you straighten up slowly and purposefully, suck in a deep breath, and pick triumphantly and delicately at one palm with the thumb and forefinger of the other hand.

'There!' you exclaim, with a relieved sigh and a grateful smile. 'Of all the places for a contact lens to drop out just as you are greeting a long-lost pal.'

Now just supposing the contact lens trick won't do it for you – given that you are sporting your glasses at the time, or that your wife is well aware that you don't wear lenses – you can either make out that you had a gruelling session with an optician that very afternoon, have discovered that you are profoundly visually challenged and the contact lenses were prescribed there and then. Or that you picked up a sudden case of river blindness while admiring the Koi carp in the patio pond. Alternatively you can affect a drunken stupor, fix your wife with a steely glare and slur,

'I have no idea who you are, sir, but allow me to introduce you to my lovely lady-wife,' as you grab luscious Lizzie – by the arm is probably safest – and pull her towards you.

Failing all else, go for The Sting.

'A wasp,' you shrug, a wrinkle of distaste distorting your mouth as you fling an imaginary insect to the floor and stamp murderously at the carpet. 'Good thing I was here – the poor girl could have been stung from the inside out by now.'

CASE NUMBER ❷: I'M AWFULLY SORRY, OFFICER, BUT . . .

You are hurtling down the road at full pelt, 9 a.m. and late for work again, sweat pumping from every pore, jumping red lights and overtaking everything in sight – including that furtive police car smoothing its way along the inside. Yes, dammit, the one that you simply didn't see.

'It's my pet badger, Officer,' you wail, hot tears pricking at your eyelids and mascara coursing down your cheeks (for some unexplained reason this seems to work better if you are female) as he or she prepares to book you (yet again) for exceeding the speed limit.

'Balthasar – that's my pet badger – he was so sick this morning and I was trying to get him to the vet. . . I had him on the back seat, and I just didn't realise that I'd left the window open, and we pulled up at the lights back there. . . and, well, he jumped ship. Just threw himself out of the window and legged it. There he goes! That way! Follow that badger!' (Sob. Gasp.)

Few officers of the law are stony-hearted enough not to respond favourably to such a moving story. Indeed, most will happily set off into the bushes on your behalf, cooing at the greenery as they go. 'Balthasar – here boy!'

Even if The Law doesn't buy the story, or has heard the badger ruse before (you're not the only one with this book you know), they will, in all likelihood, let you off, as no one likes to spend too long in the company of the insane.

CASE NUMBER ❸: DIETING

You are posing before the bedroom mirror, trying to squeeze yourself into the lilac two-piece, zips and seams a-straining, perspiration stinging your face. It's no way for a man to behave, but it's Ascot tomorrow and not a thing in your wardrobe will do up. You realise to your chagrin that the diet is once again long overdue and simply has to start now.

Diets are not to be undertaken lightly. They have to be approached sideways. Considered. Weighed up. So, in pensive mood, you take to your bed with a 2lb box of Cadbury's Milk Tray, a 3lb tub of chocolate fudge Haagen Daz and a bottle of champagne. You snatch up a notebook and pen, all your dieting manuals and articles ripped from Sunday papers which tell you about things like 'How To Shed Ten Pounds In Ten Days on a diet of nothing but walnuts and ginger beer,' and start to write. . .

Not so fast. First you take a huge swig of fizz and a mouthful of chocolate and then you start to write. The reasons for dieting just pour out of you and on to the page (unlike the pounds, it may be added – nothing's that easy).

*   I can't get into my clothes
*   I can't even get into my partner's clothes
*   I'm fed up with wearing a three-piece suit on the beach
*   I haven't seen my toe-nails for years
*   My flab's making me seasick/keeps making me fall in the road
*   All this chocolate is giving me spots

Now this column is all well and proper, but the highly trained excuser's mind will fight back and you will start to hear a different voice whispering in your ear. There are, as is often said, two sides to every strawberry. . .er story.

In a second column you write (LARGE and **in bold**):

* Dieting isn't fair on my wife – why should she give up her suet pudding?
* You know what it's like when you've got a houseful of kids to feed, it's impossible to diet.
* Weight is not always a bad thing; a guy needs a little ballast in a high wind. Dorothy was thin and look what happened to her – one gust and she's 5,000 miles from Kansas.
* I'm going through a rough patch at the moment, and if I give up eating I know I'll just start smoking again, and then I'll have to give up, which means more snacking and putting on more weight, so what's the point?
* It's fashionable to carry a little weight nowadays – you don't want people thinking you're a Supermodel or anything.
* My stomach makes a fine book-rest in bed.
* One day the Rubens look will return.
* If chocolate eclairs are so sinful, then why did God invent the cow, the cocoa bean and the food processor?

And so on. The mind is a cunning ally, and always comes to the rescue when faced with a real emergency. It may invent further, more artful reasons for abandoning the very idea of a diet, because we all know that the only way to lose weight is to stop eating and drinking so much, and to take some exercise.

And that's just not on the cards, is it?

You know what will happen the week after you start dieting. You'll be invited to the Ambassador's Ball, the liqueurs will be coming round, and men in tights will thrust Ferrero Rocher balls in your face – and what are you supposed to do, for Christ's sake, look churlish and refuse? Likewise, the port and cheese? Think of the diplomatic fall-out! Please!

And what about those dinner party scenarios where the hostess swans in, gushing, 'I made these especially for you, I know how much you love larks' tongues in lard.' What are you supposed to do, offend your hostess for the sake of nothing more important than your own vanity?

You might as well face it, it is impossible to not eat and drink and yet still socialise successfully. OK, well it's hard – and requires the sternest discipline. There's nothing worse than being out to dinner somewhere, surrounded by a bunch of degenerates whom you recognise, for once, to be your closest friends. These peasants are getting more and more sloshed, and seem, to you, increasingly ridiculous and lewd. You are bored stiff with gargling Perrier and rushing off to queue for the loo every five minutes. What's more, how the hell can you live with yourself? By not partaking of the feast, you're making them feel guilty for enjoying their food. How many hard-core calories are you actually going to save by not having a starter anyway?

The last straw comes when you split the bill at the end, and it dawns on you that you still have to pay for a sixth of all that you haven't consumed. Images of your friends grazing on the contents of your wallet pass before your eyes. In pursuing your diet, all you have achieved is the creation of a climate of mistrust, jealousy, avarice and greed. It is quite possible that, as you leave the restaurant still starving and watch the plump forms of the people-of-the-night going about their business, your thoughts will also turn to murder and cannibalism. Mmm. Yum!

So how does it all end ? In tears, of course. You go home and wolf down a whole packet of digestives and a bottle of Stoli. Thus, in one fell swoop you ruin your sleep pattern, destroy your relationship and you know your work will suffer, your kids will hate you, and your dog will run off with the postman. Fact is, nobody likes living with a misery in denial with furtive eating habits.

Stop dieting. Now. Dieting is a hazard to your health which must be taken very seriously. It is, after all, possible to trace back the cause of innumerable disasters throughout history and lay the blame firmly at the door of The Diet. To name but a few:

* The demise of the marriage of their RHs the Prince and Princess of Wales.
* Naomi Campbell's famous fall on the Paris catwalk (had she not been so thin, maybe the scrawny ankles wouldn't have buckled above the weight of those Vivienne Westwood shoes).
* The Wall Street Crash (just picture all those half-starved hokey brokers – too weak to float a good deal for want of a decent meal).
* The break-up of the Beatles (they, of course, existed on the Hippy Diet, peace-love-dope. A loaf or two's worth of cheese and pickle sandwiches and the odd meat pudding, and they might well have gone the distance. We will never know.)

See what I mean? So have another drink. Buy a bigger dress/suit/tent. Let out some buttons. Go out and have some fun. Make sure you stand next to bigger people. Make firm friends with fatties. Ask your thin friends to wear padding under their clothes when they come round. Better still, start pumping anabolic steroids into their lemon sorbets – sit back and watch your pals balloon before your very eyes. Soon, you will not be alone. As Confucius never said, 'The empty belly always finds an excuse for eating.' Amen to that.

Finally, if fatness is a state of mind, then OK, consider insanity as an option. Life's too short to say no to a stuffed mushroom.

If you're caught talking to a stuffed mushroom, see page 156.

CASE NUMBER ❹: SORRY I'M LATE...

It's the morning you get out of bed the wrong side and it's all downhill from there. OK – let's be honest, you completely overslept. Last night you managed to consume an unknown quantity of lager and a jar of pickled onions, and you may or may not have had a vindaloo.

You have an important meeting. You are speeding through the suburbs at top speed, the air-conditioning is wrestling valiantly with your every exhalation. You open a couple of windows. The car sighs with audible relief. Meanwhile you are desperately trying to think of all the excuses you haven't yet used at the office. Even worse, today it's your meeting – you are doing the presentation. You are doomed.

You screech up to the office building, brake a little late and park nattily in the middle of reception. You fly up the stairs six or seven at a time, and stare through the glass doors of the meeting room to see them all waiting for you. The chairman's red in the face, and the clients are standing up and starting to pack their briefcases. What do you do?

Only fools rush in, and you know better.

Withdraw to the privacy of your own office for a few moments and collect your thoughts. Don't go in hot-headed – it never works. Try screaming a lot. Any better? No – didn't think it would be.

Next, have your secretary bring you a couple of mugs of hot coffee, which you can either swallow or tip all over yourself in order to create some sort of diversion.

What else? You're starting to sweat a lot now. You have been the victim of a road rage incident? That's it! You got in the way of some roguish-looking guys who were on their way back from an armed robbery, and they would have made absolute mincemeat of you had not that nice young lady intervened on your behalf...no, no that won't do.

Much better to try one of the following:

I. PASS THE BUCK

Swan into the boardroom and speak first. 'Sorry to interrupt your meeting, gentlemen, but has anyone seen my colleague Joe Ninety? There's a phone call for him. I understood he was chairing this meeting this morning, and. . . What do you mean ? No, no, not my meeting, no, Joe insisted on taking this one himself . . .' (It is best to resist the temptation to grin fiendishly at this point.)

2. FAKE AN ATTACK

Try beating yourself up in the elevator and lying there covered in blood until you are discovered. Don't use the Goods and Services elevator – you might be lying there for days. Oh, and remember not to wear your best suit.

3. CREATE A DIVERSION

Set fire to the office. Extreme, but it works. You then rescue the chairman's secretary from certain death. He is probably having an affair with her anyway, and will be so grateful to you for saving her pretty little ass that he'll probably give you anything – Head of Department promotion, top-of-the-range car, transfer to New York, cruise on the QE2. If he's not having an affair with her, a fire could provide you with the excuse you've been looking for to effect an introduction. Clever, eh? It's a win-win situation in Excuse-Ville.

4. LIE

Anything relating to a pet badger (or raccoon or wombat) should do the trick – e.g. he was lying asleep on the back seat of your car, he woke up, something startled him and he hurled himself at the windscreen, just as you were taking a sip of hot black coffee from a polystyrene mug – you know the sort of thing. . .

EXCUSES, EXCUSES GALORE

OK, so you're getting the hang of it now. Let's look more closely at a few specific situations in which the art of the excuse can play a rich and varied part.

MARRIAGE AND RELATIONSHIPS

In this area perhaps more than any other, you know only too well that you will always be walking a tightrope over a piranha-infested pool. This is mainly because you can never, ever account for the mood/hormones/hidden agenda/attitude of the other person and they probably know your every thought. There is a permanent tension, and changing, shifting sands. What's more, there is no truth – only perspective. Or, as somebody once said, in any relationship there are three sides to every story: his, hers, and the truth. Come to think of it, in a relationship involving celebrities, make that four sides, because there is also the press to consider.

All of which tells you why everyone in a relationship needs excuses so badly; there is more at stake, more to gain, more to lose. In the worst-case scenario you may wind up mislaying your marbles, questioning constants, falling prey to digressional thoughts: if the world is so round, how come I keep getting backed into so many corners?

Given that the world of marriage and relationships is such a passionate and fundamental place, making the necessary excuses will require tact, charm, sensitivity and affection, plus skilful application of any or all of the techniques listed on pages 24-25. Good luck.

FORGETTING YOUR ANNIVERSARY

Apologies, but I think you'll agree that it's usually the man at fault here. 'Oh, my God' is simply not good enough. It's got to be way more inventive than that, and perhaps as far-fetched as you can possibly manage:

✱   I did buy you a bouquet, darling, but it was consumed by an Irish wolf-hound on my way up the hill.

✱   Garrards couldn't finish the ring in time, but we'll go together to collect it on Saturday. (Warning: this one could cost you dearly.)

✱   You thought I'd forgotten, didn't you? I was just waiting to see if you had! (At this point, hide in the bathroom with your mobile phone and hastily book a table at your most expensive local restaurant, taking care to order the lot: red roses on the table, vintage champagne, umbrellas in the cocktail, singing waiters, etc.)

REFUSING A DATE

You are actually refusing a date? Think yourself lucky. If you're serious, there is always our old friend Cervantes and his magical line about working late at the office (see page 10). Or you could consider the following:

* Legal complications: you have just entered into an arranged marriage, and the Home Office are on to you. If pushed, affect some exotic nationality.

* The 'application of uncertainty' ruse. 'Dinner?' you gush. 'Why, that would be lovely. When? ... Tuesday? Can't make it. Friday? Sorry – no can do. Next week? Blast – I'm away on a course.' After he/she/it has tried a dozen suggestions, all of which you have managed to dodge, you smile serenely/look wildly enthusiastic (or both if you can manage it, but it takes practice) and wait for the 64,000 dollar question: 'When, then?' To which you reply, 'I haven't got my diary on me. . . I'll call you!'

Working on the basis that we meet everybody in life twice, you must have Part Two of this excuse at the ready for the next time you bump into each other:

'How marvellous to see you again. I was devastated when I lost your number.' You did, of course, take the precaution of making sure that they gave it to you on a matchbook or shred of paper – something inflammable, digestible or easily blown away. And if the next time round he insists on writing it on your arm, don't panic. What does he think – you don't wash?

If they are insistent, they will of course ask for your number, in which case, if you really are not keen, you simply change one digit. If you're caught out later on you can claim that you are numerically dyslexic – it came on suddenly last year, 5991. Or give them your old number (you can always say that you were drunk or homesick at the time), as long as none of your friends are still living there.

Or try 'I've just moved into a new house and I'm not on the phone/haven't memorised the number yet.'

In a real emergency, you might have to resort to putting the frighteners on your persecutor – 'Actually, I'm on day-release from Holloway/Broadmoor/Alcatraz, and they don't let me out at nights.'

You won't see them for dust.

GETTING OUT OF A DATE YOU'VE ALREADY ARRANGED

You should have gone on that assertiveness course and mastered the art of saying no, because you have agreed to go on a date with someone you really don't fancy. Well, you couldn't bear to hurt his feelings face to face/you didn't want to embarrass her in front of other people, and what is worse – you just couldn't think of a decent excuse on the spot.

As the dreaded day looms, you wrack your brains for a plausible get-out; something that lets you neatly off the hook while sparing their feelings. So far, you simply haven't had the heart to call.

Right. Tonight's the night, and it's time to take the bull by the horns. You will either have to grin and bear it, wash and go, or (big breath) make a last-minute phone call which summons every ounce of your imagination. Be brave. There is real creative scope here, not to mention unlimited use of the excuser's most loyal prop: the telephone. You can blush the deepest beetroot if you like while weaving your filthy web of deceit, for no one will ever know.

Most people have a wealth of suitable excuses at their fingertips –

* Babysitter/dogsitter is sick/let me down at the last minute.
* Child is ill.
* Dog is ill.
* Child and dog are both ill.
* I am ill (anything to do with Digestive Problems will normally put anyone off a date).

✳   I've got to go to the Caribbean first thing in the morning on a job.

– but if you take pride in your excusing ability it may be time to start thinking more laterally. Try getting your tongue round some of the following – see how they fit.

✳   I don't know how to put this: I've just found a body in the cupboard. No, don't worry, thanks, the police are on their way. No . . . nobody we know.

✳   I've got to polish the ashtrays/sharpen my umbrella/tidy my paperclips/change the goldfish's water (wonderfully insulting if you've got to the stage of not giving a damn about the other person's feelings).

✳   Got a bone in my leg (for some reason my grandad got away with this one for years).

✳   Tonight? Oh, damn, I thought it was next week. I've written it in the wrong week of my diary. How stupid of me. (Dodgy, that one, because if he's free next week, you're in schtook. Better to pretend that you thought your date was last week and that you turned up, waited and waited, and have only just plucked up courage to call now – it has taken you a week to recover from deep feelings of rejection, which is why it is too soon for you to see each other again. You'll call him in a month or two.)

✳   My stars say I shouldn't go outside the door today.

✳   I've just seen five magpies in a row, so I'm staying in – sorry.

✳   I've got to go on an Animal Rights demo at short notice.

✳   I left the bleach on my hair too long and I've gone bald/green/purple.

✳   I put hot wax on my legs and it set really hard, and I couldn't bring myself to rip it off, so now I've got to wait for my flatmate/cleaning lady/cat to arrive so that I can get them to chip it off with a screwdriver.

✱ The cat fell in the hot wax, and I'm waiting for the vet.

✱ I've Superglued my fingers together – no, it's worse than it sounds, you have no idea where I had them at the time. . .

✱ We're having a bit of a *crise de famille* . . .my sister's just walked out on her old man, and she's turned up here with the five kids and a German Shepherd. . . no, it's a dog, actually. . .anyway, it's looking a bit like the fourth form dorm around here at the moment, sleeping bags everywhere, and the dog's insisting on a bowl of sauerkraut.

✱ I've just gone into labour (no need to specify whether you are talking party politically, procreatively or about your recent visit to the Job Centre: the mere word is enough to dampen the most ardent of suitors).

✱ Please bear with me, I'm suffering from concussion and temporary loss of memory. . . who did you say I was again?

✱ I know it's a bit short notice to call off our date at the eleventh hour, but that's what it's there for, you see. Otherwise, we'd find ourselves going directly from the tenth hour to the twelfth – and then where would we be?

✱ I had a close encounter with a foaming fire extinguisher on the train home. No, they can't tell me how long the blindness will last.

✱ This is rather embarrassing, actually, but I appear to have acquired an, erm, infestation. (Keep it nebulous and non-specific – lice ain't nice.)

✱ Well, it looks like a common or garden cold sore to me, but you can never tell these days, can you?

✱ I've had an adverse reaction to the prawns in liquorice I tried last night, and I'm covered in the most awful livid orange blotches.

✱ How can I put this – I've posted my false teeth by mistake. . . I know, they're good, aren't they, nobody can ever tell. Anyway, I've got to go back there and wait by the mailbox until Postman Pat shows up.

✱ I'm in mourning . . . I've just destroyed my prize Pacific orchid collection with the remote-control lawnmower.

✱ I've just come home from work to find that someone's nicked eighteen vests, three bath hats and eleven pairs of knickers off my washing line, and I haven't got a thing to wear.

✱ I'm completely lame. . . I was sitting on the toilet in a public convenience, when a hand appeared under the door and pinched my shoes. I had to hobble home barefoot, cobbled streets all the way, wouldn't you know it, just my luck. . .'

Or perhaps you could call their bluff, suggest an activity guaranteed to put them off:

* I don't know about you but I really fancy going swinging tonight: you know, a little recreational sex with a whole bunch of strangers? You, me and whoever we can pick up down the pub. You know – girls, boys, whatever, as long as they seem reasonably clean. How about it?

Come to think of it, that one's risky unless you know them well enough to be sure they *will* be put off.

Failing all else, there is always a Technicolored version of 'The Truth':

I'm not feeling very celibate tonight Susan so I better stay at home where I can keep an eye on myself

✱ I've decided to act on the advice of my therapist for once, and be honest with myself about my unrealistic expectations of relationships and love. So, I'm sorry, but I'm going to have to let you down. It's not your fault – it's nothing you've done, and you don't smell or anything – it's just that I'm establishing a new beginning for myself. Restructuring my foundations. Regrouping my energies. I hope you understand. You wouldn't want to be with such a person anyway. Transition is pain.

In the unlikely event that none of these has the desired effect (goodness, you sure pick the thick-skinned ones, don't you?), and they are brazen enough to turn up on your doorstep, you will have to do something pretty drastic such as throwing yourself down the stairs. The true professional will have a plaster cast at the ready (here's one I made earlier), and perhaps even keep it strategically placed behind the front door, ready to dive straight into.

REJECTING A PASS

Let's face it, making a pass in the first place is not very PC these days. But since when did political correctness count for anything in matters sexual? If you are under 35 you probably find the whole mating ritual a bit of a bore anyway – you wish they wouldn't, and you plan to give the next one who comes on to you a good slapping (although not too good, they might just be into that sort of thing).

Over 35 and you are practically begging for it. Life's too short to refuse lawful pleasures. But you still want to be able to choose your partner.

Anyway, assuming the pass has been made, and you wouldn't be seen dead with this one, the job in hand is to get out of it, and fast. The more predictable tactics include:

* Sorry, wrong time of the month (more effective if you are female).
* I'm afraid I'm suffering from an obscure sexual disease (ensure that no one you might remotely fancy overhears this).
* I'm very flattered, but I have to tell you that I'm gay – or straight, if you actually are gay. (A word of caution: this can be the proverbial scarlet hankie to male bovine in the case of the truly red-blooded predator of either gender, who will regard it as a challenge and possibly attempt to convert you. Under no circumstances step outside with such a person.)

There is probably no harm in claiming that you may soon, allegedly, have the opportunity to bring Mike Tyson to trial for attempted date rape; that you are a bitter and twisted misandrist/misogynist as a result of your five failed marriages; or that you are actually a plant for Blind Date/Beadle's About/Candid Camera and the stunt about to be, um, pulled on four concealed cameras is so cringe-making that in your opinion the best bet would be to shift your rear to a more suitable venue, on the double.

On the other hand, you could smile sweetly, flap your lashes, accept the offer of a drink and order a bottle of nicely chilled Dom Perignon 1965, none of your House rubbish. Sip delicately at a glass of it before excusing yourself to go to the Ladies' room; then you climb out of the toilet window, leg it up the street and never come back. If you were in the company of good friends prior to the pass, scrawl them a lipstick message on the bathroom mirror or leave a confidential note giving details of your revised whereabouts.

SEX!

There. . . I knew we could get your attention.

Let me just remind you, as if you didn't know, that the business of sex, or indeed no sex, in a relationship, is an absolute minefield, on to which you should venture with the utmost caution. The mere suggestion that you might try something different for once can result in one almighty explosion as your partner immediately goes either on the defensive:

*   Oh, okay, so you're telling me we've been doing it wrong all this time and it's been no bloody good for you. . .you've been faking!

Or on the offensive:

*   What's all this funny stuff? Who did you learn that one off? Put that thing away!

Tread fearfully, is the best advice, and do not attempt any of the following without lashings of humour and at least one tongue in your cheek.

I'd love to have sex, but. . .

* I've just had a bath/changed the sheets/applied my fake tan.
* I'm watching the football.
* It's not the 23rd again already, is it?
* I'm saving myself for the full moon.
* But there's an R in the month.

* But there isn't an R in the month.
* I've had an unbelievably hard day at the office (make sure you're in employment before you try this one).
* I've got a tricky game of golf in the morning, and you know what they say about great athletes never having sex before a game. (Be warned – the response to this might well be, 'But you play golf every day', to which you hit home with the classic hole-in-one: 'Precisely, dearest. I don't deserve a husband/wife like you. I'm so glad you see it my way.')

If you are a woman who has fallen into the habit of refusing her man to the point that you really can't be bothered with sex at all any more, be warned that you will only get away with Old Faithfuls such as the Headache, Time Of The Month and Just Painted The Toenails number for so long. He is bound to see through you sooner or later.

'I just don't feel sexy tonight' won't do it either: he's likely to leap on you with a lusty 'Oh yes, you do' and you'll only have yourself to blame. Why not try something along the lines of:

✱ Well, darling, women are such complicated and sensitive creatures, and it's less to do with the body than the mind, and I'm so sorry, look it's not you, but the thing is, I'm way too fertile, and I'll get pregnant if you just look at me, and I prefer my eggs at breakfast to be unfertilised, no, you know I'm allergic to rubber. . . waffle, waffle, waffle, until you bore him right to sleep.

Sometimes, though, you will find that the condom is on the other foot, as it were. You are feeling rather frisky, but your partner does not feel inclined to play ball. (Did you really join the Mile-High Club on your own on the plane home from Boston last week, or was it all a bad dream?) Forget the idea of threatening behaviour. It will never get you what you want and it might even get you arrested. Instead, try a little tenderness. Perfect the art of gentle persuasion. Just a couple of minutes should do it, if you manage not to grimace or look bored. Coo sweetly as you wrack your brain for the best excuse:

* You know I need to lose weight, darling, and did you realise it's a thousand calories a bonk?

* No, you don't need to lose weight, but this has got to be more fun than step aerobics, hasn't it?

* You know how you're always telling me it's good for the skin.

* Please, darling, you know it helps me get a really good night's sleep, and then I won't keep you awake all night with my snoring.

* I'm so tense, and let's face it: it's less effort for you than giving me a back massage.

* I know I said I was giving up – but I really need an excuse to have a cigarette.

FALLING ASLEEP AT THE WRONG MOMENT

Well, what can you say? It is the ultimate insult, particularly to a lover who has gone to great lengths to make it a truly memorable occasion. You have blown it. Then again, have you? This one should really test the excusatory skills you have acquired so far.

Here's your starter for ten. Try countering the accusation 'You were asleep!' with 'No, I wasn't!' If you've being paying even half-hearted attention to this book so far, you'll recognise that for the pathetic cop-out it is.

If you feel that something more elaborate is called for, then ad-lib, embroider, colour it in, as boldly as you dare:

* I wasn't asleep, I was in Nirvana. . . you took me there and clean forgot to bring me back.
* I was trying out some hypnosis techniques from Paul McKenna's video – for better sex, you understand – and what do you know, they work! How was it for you?

NB. If this is a persistent habit of yours, it might just be that you need a more scintillating partner. (Or, perish the thought, that your partner needs a more scintillating partner.) But if a trade-in is simply not a viable proposition, try feigning a medical condition, such as recurrent sleeping sickness that you picked up before you met, while working for a humanitarian aid programme in the Niger Delta/Thames Estuary/Barossa Valley.

An excuse of this variety requires continual up-keep. Cultivate the habit of falling asleep at other odd times during the day while you are not making love. Run the risk, go the whole hog, do it in places detrimental to your health and reputation and they can't help but believe you. But if you fall asleep with your head in the soup at dinner, first ensure that said soup is not too hot. The really advanced excuser could then pretend to wake up, rise dripping from the minestrone dish, look vacantly around and say, 'How the hell did all these people get in my bedroom?' or 'Darling, you're dressed.' You could also get yourself into the habit of not finishing sentences, such as, 'There I was at the hole in the wall, just about to draw out two hundred and fifty in cash, when . . . zzzzz.'

MARRIAGE - AND HOW TO AVOID IT

First of all, if you are male with a pierced ear, remove the earring right away. You are perceived by the female of the species to be well-prepared for marriage: you have experienced pain and bought jewellery.

There's no easy way to tell your long-term partner/live-in lover that you simply don't want to marry them. Whatever you say is bound to hurt them deeply. On that basis, you can either go for the jugular, be irredeemably offensive when cornered and console yourself with the fact that at least you won't ever have to see them again. . .trouble is, you would quite like to see them again. There was nothing wrong with the relationship in the first place – apart from the fact that you didn't want to legalise it at gross expense. Why bother?

If you can't face wounding the gentle creature who has remained devoted to you for so long, you are going to have to work on a cracking excuse that will not only save their face and preserve the status quo but also get you off the hook.

Firstly, establish the real reason for not wanting to get married before starting to plan the gentle let-down. Take your time, be honest with yourself. Is it that you quite like the comfort and relative security of living with someone, but you also wish to maintain the illusion of being single and enjoy your relative freedom? Could it be that you are not averse to the idea of marriage, per se, you would just rather marry someone else? Do you want to keep your options open at the moment? Have you a sneaking suspicion that there is someone out there somewhere who is more 'right' for you? Or is it simply that you don't want to share your toys?

Once you have established your own attitude towards marriage, you can go about the business of selecting an excuse to match.

* Nothing personal, just a question of keeping my options open.
* Nothing personal, just a question of keeping *your* options open.
* I *know* it's selfish, but I just want to have you all to myself. If we get married, the next thing you know your mother and my mother and the cat's mother will be getting on to us to have kids. You may not think so now but the broody thng *will* get to you. I'm making it my responsibility to prevent that from happening to you. I love you far too much.
* I guess we could give it a whirl. I've always wanted to have a go at that bit from *The Graduate* where the bride jilts the fiancé at the altar and jumps a bus into the sunset with Dustin Hoffman – what do you say?
* It just won't work for me. The last time I got hitched I had to rush out and have several simultaneous death-wish marriage-threatening affairs. You'd rather have a faithful lover than a love-rat spouse, surely to God?

✳   It's like this: I once met this woman in Las Vegas: Charlotte Richards, Wedding Queen of the West. Straight up, true story, she did 50-odd weddings a day. And they *were* odd, too. Slid down waterfalls doing it, jumped out of planes doing it, the whole shooting match. She owned chapels, parlours, marriage temples, even this little Drive-Thru place where you could get married in two minutes without even getting out of your car. Mercenary or what? Whole thing was sick. Put me right off. Worse than that, it cheapened the very concept of marriage for me: where was the sanctity, the ceremony, the considered commitment, the Love-Honour-Obey, the stag night, the build up, the leg up, the throw up? I'm telling you now, it's going to take some years, a lot of dough and mucho therapy to work this thing out. If, on the other hand, you're not in any kind of hurry we could talk about it again in ten years...

✳   Sure, let's do it. My lifelong ambition is to get married while abseiling down the Matterhorn in a transparent turquoise body suit as the preacher reads extracts from *Gone with the Wind*. What *is* the matter, horn. . .I mean, hon?

✳   Frank Sinatra and the rest of those loony croonies got it wrong. Love and marriage! Love and marriage, my foot. When did *you* last see a horse with an undercarriage?

✳   Lemmingsville, USA: so what you're telling me is you're not enough of an individual to take a stance against something all your friends are doing, right? Mark my words, sunshine, we'll be drinking to their divorces in a couple of years.

✳   You, in white?

Or there's the defensive approach:

✱ I'm actually addicted to the idea of being a complete slob of a bachelor/spinster. I like being able to wear my underwear more than once, leave the toilet seat up/down without feeling guilty and live in this appalling shambles of a home without having anyone scream at me. In short: I like my miserable life!

If all else fails, and only as a last resort, you might have to fall back on Putting Yourself Down:

✱ I'm just not good enough for you. . . you're bound to find somebody better than me, without nearly so many disgusting habits and faults. (Tread carefully here – he/she might recognise the truth when they hear it and decide to move on.)

65

INFIDELITY

The trousers are not only down and under starter's orders, they're off. So is every other shred of your attire. You are horizontally positioned, give or take, above or below a rather delectable young specimen of the opposite sex, and about to partake of some fascinating Ugandan discussions, when in walks your other half.

In flagrante delicto, they call this one. Literally, caught red-handed (and red everywhere else, by the looks of things). What's a poor adulterer to do?

You are thinking, 'I know how this looks. . .' And it does, I'm afraid, it really does. There is little point in wasting time on run-of-the-mill get-out clauses or niceties. This is a dire emergency, and requires an excuse of the highest imaginative order.

Something like:

* Oh, Miranda! It seems I had rather taken leave of my senses for a moment. I imagined I was beside a blue lagoon on a parched afternoon. I must have flung off all my clothes ready to dive in, when suddenly I woke up and saw you standing there. . . I don't know, who is she?
* Actually, darling, I was trying to keep it as a surprise. . . I've been doing an Open University degree in Anatomy, and this is part of the practical. Just delivered this morning, so I thought I'd get on with it while you were out.
* After all, dearest, as Thomas Hardy once said, 'A lover without indiscretion is no lover at all.' (Better not to mention Oscar Wilde, who reckoned that the only way to get rid of temptation was to yield to it).

* Bed, as the Italian proverb succinctly puts it, is the poor man's opera (the fact that she won't have a clue what this means should get you off the hook).
* Ah, darling, I forgot to mention – I'm doing some homework to make our own lovemaking more satisfying. Those nice marriage guidance people advised it, but I really don't enjoy it one bit, and what's more it's costing me five hundred quid an hour.

Or, pretend that you are the whore:

* How do you think I've been paying all these bills/school fees recently? And you went and bought Stephanie that pony, and Jamie a new Harley Davidson for his birthday, and money doesn't grow on trees, you know. Then turn to your lover and say, 'That'll be £500, please – how will you be paying?'

Of course, not all adulterers are so stupid as to indulge in sexual activity of the prohibited kind in their own homes, or any other location where they are likely to be discovered by their partner. But infidelity is a danger zone and no mistake. Enter at your peril.

If you are a young, impressionable female embroiled in an affair with an older, very married man, you are probably already making excuses to yourself, such as 'He loves me.' Oh, no, he doesn't. I'll tell you what he is, darling: addicted to your springy flesh. He just wants to get away with having his cake and eating it for as long as possible. He has no intention of leaving his wife for you.

If you're the one having a little extra-curricular, you will have been giving your dewy-eyed paramour a number of your finest excuses as to why you need her but can't be with her:

* My wife doesn't understand me/we simply grew apart. (NB If you are the dewy-eyed paramour on the receiving end of this – don't fall for it. She understands him only too well.)
* The affection has gone out of our relationship/we never do it any more (which you can get away with until your wife falls pregnant. You then say that it must be by another man).
* I was celibate, unfulfilled for years, until I met you. (NB to the dewy-eyed paramour – this is bullshit. Unfulfilled maybe. Celibate? Do me a favour!)
* We're only staying together for the sake of the children.
* She's the one with the money.

When he is discovered as the miserable two-timer of a rat that he is, he will tell his wife the following:

* It was nothing.
* It was only once.
* I never meant you to find out.

* I don't love them. . . whoops, I mean, her!
* It just happened.
* We were drunk.

✳   I was doing it with her but thinking of you.

Some of these may even be true, but as we have established, the truth is a poor substitute for a good excuse.

Meanwhile, the wronged wife is also making excuses to herself. She may even be in denial: 'This isn't happpening. It's all a bad dream. If I close my eyes it will all go away. It'll be all right in the morning.'

BREAKING UP

This is so hard to do. . .where is Neil Sedaka when you want him? You know it's going to hurt, but they will get over it. Life goes on. So get that needle in their arm, push the plunger and get out – fast.

✳   I'm just no good for you. I'm holding you back.

✳   You know I can't commit myself.

✳   There'd be no place for you in the Cistercian monastery.

✳   I've seen the light/got God.

MAKING A PASS AT SOMEONE ELSE'S PARTNER

You will only need to make excuses about this if the Someone Else turns out to be your boss's husband or wife, your best friend's new partner or a member of your partner's family whom you just didn't recognise. The best way out is to feign drunkenness and make a quick getaway – forget about despatching bouquets of apology the next day, this would only be tightening your own noose. But supposing you are a confirmed teetotaller – nah, you wouldn't be reading a sleazy book like this if you were. However, there are always exceptions to the rule, and I guess you might prove to be one of them. In that case, an over-generous swig of communion wine, an intoxicating sniff of an alcohol-based perfume or the prevailing wind coming from the glue factory may have to be your excuse.

If, on the other hand, your own partner has caught you in the act, please refer to Case History Number 1 (page 28).

CHILDREN

Children are hereditary. If your parents didn't have any, chances are you won't either.

Seriously, though, to have or have not? That is the question.

If you did not have this conversation before you married/moved in together, more fool you. But what if you did have the conversation and one of you has now changed your mind?

REASONS FOR NOT HAVING THEM

* It would ruin my figure.
* The stretch marks around my mouth are bad enough.
* There's a population explosion . . . think how many kids there'll be on the planet by the year 2000.
* It's ridiculously hard to find decent schools these days.
* We've got two cats already. Think how jealous they'd get with babies in the house. It wouldn't be safe.
* I had a tragic childhood. Having kids will bring it all back for me, and we can't afford the therapy.
* That would mean we'd have to have sex (again).

REASONS FOR HAVING THEM

✱   Well, after all, we are married, aren't we?

✱   My mother and your mother and the biddy in the sub-post office keep asking when we're going to start a family.

✱   I don't want people around here thinking there's something wrong with us, you know, down *there*.

✱   All our friends seem to have children and it feels like we no longer have anything in common with them.

✱   All these years we've been forking out for presents for an army of godchildren; isn't it about time we got something back?

✱   I can see myself wanting to take time to smell the roses with my grandchildren in years to come and you have to make some sort of an investment in all that *now*.

✱   Well, *you* won't play football with me.

If you've already got them, then you need another category of excuse, viz

REASONS FOR NOT DEALING WITH THEM
Try sucking up to your partner with lines like

* You're the only one they respond to.
* They don't have any respect for me.
* But I've no patience and you're so lovely with them.
* I'm feeling terribly aggressive tonight, I just don't trust myself. (Quite plausible, given that most of the time you think they are undisciplined, foul-mouthed little rogues.)
* It's not my turn.

EXCUSES START YOUNG
There isn't a kid alive who hasn't made excuses to its parents. Think about it: when did you first start spinning lines to yours? Don't you just cringe when you think about the kind of whoppers you fed them, poor, unsuspecting things? Difference is, you probably didn't get into it until you were a budding teenager – the age when you start having thoughts and desires to get guilty about. Nowadays they begin everything so much younger. They're barely out of Pampers before their little minds are corrupted (by television, mostly, or by books like this, sometimes) and their tongues start dripping with porky pies. I include this section both as a revision course to parents and in order to set the under-age excusers among us on their merry way. After all, everyone's got to start somewhere.

NB to kids dipping into this book: if Mum or Dad catches you with their copy, you weren't reading it, just looking at the pretty pictures, OK?

HOMEWORK

So much to do, so little time, and the question as to why you aren't doing your homework keeps cropping up. However, you are prepared.

✳   Academic work is not my bag. I'm more of an artisan.

✳   I've decided to leave school and enter a convent. (Most effective if you're Jewish or Seventh Day Adventist, but worth a try even if you're not.)

✳   I'm manically depressed about the ecological state of the globe and I just can't concentrate.

✳   I have to watch TV right now. I'm doing a thesis on soap operas/sport in the media/youth culture.

SCHOOL REPORTS

Parents have great expectations of their offspring, and every generation is supposed to exceed the achievements of the one before. So the moment when the school report hits the mat – or, worse still, has to be handed over in person, so you can't arrange to be miles away – requires some forethought and perhaps the use of some pre-emptive pre-cuses in the days leading up to its arrival. Such as:

*   You know our teacher left half way through the term to have a baby? Well, the new guy's a jerk, completely useless. How we're supposed to get on in the world with a mentor like that, I just don't know. God help us when the reports come out.
*   The science teacher has a grudge against me, ask anyone. He's going to give me bad marks out of spite.
*   I could swear that the maths teacher is jealous of my intelligence and natural good looks. Can I help it if I've got everything going for me? I just hope they don't hold it against me when it really counts.
*   You're not going to believe this, but the teacher made a pass at me, and you know what they say about a woman scorned.

When the dark day comes, prepare to trot out the following. At least some of the above should have worked, so your parents may be sympathetic as well as sceptical.

*   Everybody did badly this year, the results were really poor overall.
*   Look on the bright side. I'm top of my class at differential equations! We

✱   just didn't get examined on them this year.

✱   But this isn't my report! I know I was top in art and social biology. They must have mixed me up with someone else.

If you see that these fine and just reasons are falling on deaf ears, you could always try preying on their greatest fears: tell them about your involvement in a teenage pregnancy; of your passionate involvement with a married man who is not to blame for the failure of his three previous marriages; of your conversion to shamanism, and of the money you owe your drug dealer. Watch their faces turn an interesting shade of ash. See them start to shake with the immenseness of it all, and then tell them that none of it is true after all; that you just wanted to put your poor school report into some sort of perspective.

PARENTS, AND HOW TO GET AWAY FROM THEM

Finding a good excuse to fly the nest on a regular basis is a must for any budding excuser. Be generous – make them feel you're doing it for them.

✱   It's high time you guys had some time on your own to, er, listen to records (to the uninitiated, that's a quaint old euphemism for having sex).

✱   I wouldn't want to bore you too much with. . . (then blind them with the latest hip-hop, top-of-the-pop, outtasight, uptight, web-site, superhighway techno-jargon, whatever you call it these days, and bore them to sleep so you can go out without them even noticing).

✱   You've always done so much for me, the least I can do is go out partying tonight and give you the place to yourselves.

✳   I'd love to stay home tonight but I'll be out doing community service/gardening for old folk/shopping for invalids/helping out at the youth club.

All this can also explain why your school reports have been so bad – it's because of all the quality time you've spent helping others. You're selfless, you see.

NOT INTRODUCING THE BOYFRIEND/GIRLFRIEND

At some point in our development, we all find ourselves ashamed of our parents because:

a) They are completely uncool/non-trendy/drive the wrong car; who wouldn't rather walk ten miles to school over mountainous terrain than have them take you there in that thing? *or*

b) They are embarrassingly trendy/trying to be too young for their age/your mother still shops at Miss Selfridge/dyes her hair pink and, wait for it, your dad dances . . .

So it's not surprising that you can't bear to bring your new boyfriend or girlfriend within fifty yards of your house (which may also be because your bedroom's a tip). But much as your parents get on your nips, you don't want to hurt their feelings. So you need an excuse or two. Go on, throw them a fish. Try these:

* I always have to go round to his house because his mum and dad don't let him out during the week.
* She's agoraphobic.
* She's just getting over a serious operation, and my bedside manner is doing wonders for the rehabilitation. She should be able to go out again by Christmas.
* We're working on a project together, and all the stuff's at his place.
* You know how it is, Mum: the minute I bring her home to meet you she'll start getting ideas and thinking that I'm serious about her, and wanting to get married and everything, and after all, I'm only fourteen!

The trouble with having kind, loving, but ultimately embarrassing parents is that excuses have to be presented on both fronts – having dealt with the parents, you also need to make excuses to the boyfriend or girlfriend about why you will not be inviting them over. No one likes to admit that their folks have a predilection for Rolf Harris records and the word 'cool'.

When pressed on the subject, try contorting your face; cultivate a dark, mysterious, pensive look. The implication is that there is something terribly wrong at home which you can't bring yourself to discuss. Stamping around a lot and being defensive – 'You're always asking questions, just like my bloody parents. Stop interrogating me . . .' – is a possible, if not very tactful, approach. Or you could bring out one of the above chestnuts and give it an alternative spin:

* We need to play it cool, that's all. You have no idea how heavy my parents can be. The minute they meet you they'll start thinking that this

is the Real Thing, reeeeally serious, and that we're about to get married or something, and after all we are only fourteen.

GETTING CAUGHT

Life has a little game it likes to play on the young – it shows us the way to a procession of forbidden fruits – smoking, drinking, whatever – and then smacks the hand that reaches for them. Adults Only. Us and them. The reasons for this state of affairs are pretty flimsy, but until the revolution comes we must accept things as they are and do what our parents did in the face of their parents' strictures – break the rules, taste the fruit and hope not to get busted. We should be fore-armed with a battery of excuses that we can fire across the generation gap with confidence.

* If it was good enough for Sir Walter Raleigh, it's good enough for me.
* I thought I'd take my lead from you. After all, you told me you used to smoke and drink furtively when you were my age, and look what fine people you've turned out to be.
* I'm doing a project on substance abuse, and this is part of the practical.
* Didn't I tell you I have a tapeworm? I'm trying to kill it with alcohol.
* I read somewhere that it's good for my spots.
* I'm practising to be an Angry Young Man, and I need to die before I get old. In the meantime a poet needs to do his fair share of rebelling against the Establishment and railing against the universe, as you do.
* I've had such a harmonious upbringing that I felt I needed somehow to incur your wrath, put a little aggression into my life, learn how to deal with

the bad stuff.

✳ This was the only way I could get your attention, we're just not talking lately – do you really think I got caught by accident?

WHAT TIME DO YOU CALL THIS, THEN?

It's a fact that no matter what time you get home, the parents will always be waiting up. Even if they've gone to bed, rest assured that they will still be awake and listening for your safe return. After all, it's only because they care (or because they're jealous). So if you manage to get yourself safely through the front door, quickly take all your clothes off in the hall, stuff them under the stairs and begin your ascent. If the lights go on abruptly, you can close your eyes, fling your arms out in front of you and moan 'Where am I?' in a somnambulistic monotone. Alternatively, rush into the kitchen, wrap yourself in a tea towel, plough through the contents of the fridge, quickly make a mess on the kitchen table – and pretend you've been home for hours having a midnight feast for one. Too much attention to homework is interfering with your sleep patterns and dietary requirements.

If you are actually intercepted before you can do these things, with one foot on the welcome mat, you may have to try the usual:

✳ The train was cancelled/bus was late.
✳ We had to take one of our other friends home, they live in a rough area and you are always saying that there is sufty in nambers. (Try to remain upright and not reek of booze when delivering this one.)

EXCUSES IN THE WORK PLACE

A relatively safe area, this, as everyone in the firm further up the ladder than you has been where you are now, and will have made the kind of excuses you are likely to make. Indeed, they will almost expect them. Some of them might even experience a warm glow of nostalgia as they hear the time-honoured morsels tumble from your lips. But, just to make it more lively for everyone concerned, use your imagination.

BEING LATE

Try not to rely on repetitions of the traffic news or railway station announcements. A little attention to geography also helps: 'The bridge was up' will only apply if you happen to work in a town where there is such a bridge.

Instead, go for something a little more inventive:

* I had to administer mouth-to-mouth on the station platform – this guy dropped on the ground right in front of me. Okay, I know I'm four hours late – is it my fault he looked like Brad Pitt?
* This woman on the underground had really long hair, right down to her pelvis, and as she was getting off the train, she brushed past me and got her hair tangled round one of my raincoat buttons. Well, you should have seen it, it was terrible, there she was, running frantically along the platform, knocking people over left, right and centre, and there I was with my ear welded to the glass inside the carriage and turning blue. . .thank goodness someone pulled the communication cord, otherwise what might have happened next doesn't bear thinking about . . . we wound up in hospital, still tied together, with her being treated for shock and me hanging around waiting to be cut loose. Talk about hair of the dog. . . only joking. . .no, I'm perfectly all right, absolutely, all set to do what's left of a day's work.

FALLING ASLEEP IN THE AFTERNOONS

One minute you were walking along the beach at Bali Bali, and the next you were bolt upright behind your desk, staring into the unsympathetic eyes of a disdainful

colleague. You've been snoozing again. Your boss is unimpressed, your secretary is ashamed and your peers think you're a lightweight prat. The fact is, they've all got it wrong. You're only doing it for them. . .

* I've been up all night doing this report. (Always keep one to hand.)
* I've got sleeping sickness, but I won't let you down by deserting my post.
* I wasn't sleeping, I was meditating. I only have to do three minutes a day and what a vast improvement to my concentration it makes. We should make it compulsory for all staff – think what it would do to our share value.
* Actually it's jet lag – that exhausting but rewarding business thing in Bermuda three months ago has finally caught up with me. They do say it can be a delayed reaction at my age. It'll get better after I hit 30/40/50 . . .
* This is my way of coping with the pressure, and you must admit it's better than beating up your secretary. (Your secretary will like this one.)

✱   I'm on this H_2O diet, and I keep getting dizzy . . . however, if I close my eyes and breathe deeply for ten minutes at regular intervals throughout the day, I can easily cope. Think of the benefits – I won't be so much of a liability on the company health insurance, and ultimately my work will benefit.

EXPENSES CLAIMS

This may well be the most creative writing you have done all week, but now the completed forms have landed back on your desk and you have some serious explaining to do. How can you possibly be over budget by almost a grand? Here's how:

✱   The promotions people sent me to Milan straight from the office last week while you were away, sir – good thing I had my passport on me. Of course, I had nothing with me, in terms of clothes, personal equipment, etc., but I was told just to buy everything I needed when I got there. (In other words, you succumbed to a rare and fabulous opportunity to replace your entire wardrobe in a stylish city. This won't work if the nearest you get to a foreign trip is a saunter to the newsagent's to buy paper clips.)

✱   That Junior Health Minister, God, I had to go out on the tiles with her every night for three weeks, and she only drinks single malt by the bottle.

✱   These aren't my expense claims: somebody's trying to frame me.

I COULDN'T DO THE JOB BECAUSE . . .

* The photocopier broke down (again. In most offices this will have the advantage of being true.)

* I can't type these letters because my nails are too long and I'm off to a party tonight.

* I haven't got my contact lenses.

* It's the wrong type of air in the office today.

* I've realised that I'm just not a desk person.

* I had my laptop stolen in Amsterdam (gives you a certain cachet, this one, and no one will know whether the work you should have done was on the laptop or not).

Claim sexual harassment. Don't say who it is – you don't want to get anyone into trouble, but you have been so stressed out over it . . . you are dealing with it, however, with the help of your aromatherapist/ kinesiologist/ hypnotherapist, and should be back on course in no time.

Alternatively, claim problems at home. Look embarrassed and shuffle a lot if anyone seems likely to probe too deeply.

Or there's the global view:

✱   I know I haven't finished on time, but I've been taking a more strategic view of things this past week, and I have come to the conclusion that . . .

Or:

✱   It's because I have fallen madly in love with you, and I simply can't concentrate . . . could we go out to lunch and discuss this, please?

Too long-winded? How about

✱   I want you. Now. (Smoulder, drool). Observe closely the reaction of the person to whom you address this remark. If he/she runs out of the room, you have succeeded hands down. If they seem keen, you're going to have to resort to Plan B – unless you really do fancy them, of course:

Plan B . . . There is no Plan B, be . . .because I haven't thought of one. You'll just have to work one out on your own.

THE IFS AND BUTS OF DOMESTIC BLISS

Nobody really likes housework, and anyone who claims to enjoy ironing is either lying or has a screw loose. Personally, I would rather clean eighteen filthy toilets than steam-press one linen shirt. However ironing, along with all those other thankless domestic chores, has to be done, preferably by someone else. Anyone else.

In an ideal world, we would hire a cleaning lady to do it all for us, but even this can be hazardous, not to mention expensive, and domestic staff must be chosen with the utmost care. For a start, they have to be able to do the job, not just sweep everything under the carpet, whizz round your home with a lick and a promise, hide your earrings and settle down in front of the telly with a coffee and their feet up to watch Neighbours at six pounds an hour. If you need further excuses for not hiring a decontamination operative, there is always the fear that one day, you might become famous. Will your cleaning lady start squirrelling away incriminating bits of evidence, take Polaroids of the contents of your drawers and cupboards and save your rubbish (oh, the embarrassment: those tubes of haemorrhoid cream; those blancmange-flavoured condoms), and sell her story to the popular press? Keeping things in the family will at least afford you some peace of mind (until they sell their story to the press, of course).

Doing the domestics yourself is an extreme measure, and should only be a last resort. If you live alone, you have only yourself to blame for the squalor. And maybe you enjoy wallowing in squalor. In which case, bully for you.

Things can get tricky when you live with someone else, however, because they have expectations above and beyond a share in a sink full of last week's dirty dishes, and they are apt to say noble-sounding things about a division of labour and all that twaddle. It may be your domain, or your turn, but you must either get someone else to do the housework, or find a set of reasons why it hasn't been done.

✱   I would have dusted round but I've been sneezing all day. I think I have an allergy to the housedust mite, which as you know thrives on moisture such as is found near the steam iron, the washing machine and the bed. You could say I am allergic to housework. I would.

✳ I would have made the bed, but I thought I'd mow the lawn first, and I couldn't find the key to the garden shed, which I think you had last.

✳ We've run out of Hoover bags. (Remember to stab the one in the appliance.)

✳ There was a power cut (remember to unplug the video, alarm clock, etc. so that they flash in agreement).

✳ The sun's out today – I'll do it tomorrow when it's raining.

✳ I had to sit down and pay all the bills. (You haven't actually done this because you can't find them, but with luck it will be a while before your partner discovers this.)

✳ I'm simply too tired to concentrate on doing the ironing properly, and if a thing's worth doing. . .

✳ I was in the garage looking for the iron, and when I couldn't find it, I went to come back indoors and found I couldn't get out because the electronic door had jammed itself shut. I've been in there all day. (How you got out is an area best left to those with a PhD in excuse-making.)

✳ I got locked out of the house this morning, I had to go to the pub to use the toilet, and somehow I wound up staying there for lunch . . . you know how it is . . .

Alternatively, you can take a leaf out of my friend Al's book and invent a phobia. It's baffling and ultimately meaningless, for sure, but the beauty of it is, there's no answer to it.

ON RUNNING OUT OF MILK/TOILET PAPER

Milk and loo paper are considered to be the basic requirements for an ordered home. If you run out of them, it says a lot about your state of mind, not to mention your home-making skills. Your name will start to be heard in low places, such as supermarkets, as a euphemism for social decay. It is therefore wise to have some mitigating remarks ready should the worst occur, and before the word gets out.

* I've been robbed ! Get on to the police, tell them that we are looking for a ne'er-do-well with dysentery and a calcium deficiency!

* I don't know where it all goes, I'm sure we've got a poltergeist. I only went shopping on Monday.

* It's that cranky old woman up the road, she nicks the bottles off our step and feeds our milk to her cats.

* I have an over-active golden retriever puppy with a great thirst, and who could deny such limpid eyes ? There he goes, follow that loo roll!

* I've decided not to buy toilet paper any more, as I've just thought of a great way to recycle our newspapers . . . what's more, it'll save us the weekly trip to the dump.

PETS

You love the dog and the cat, and sometimes taking the dog for a walk is a great pleasure. Sometimes it is a useful excuse and cover for another activity. Sometimes it's just too much like hard work. Cleaning out the cat litter tray is a different matter, to be avoided at all times. Best to be prepared on both counts:

* I thought the cat tray was clean. I mean it looks clean. . .what do you mean, they bury it?
* But isn't the cat tray self-cleaning, like the cat?
* The dog's asleep. I couldn't bring myself to wake him.
* I would have taken Rover out, but there are disturbing reports of high concentrations of low-level ozone. He'd only suffer.

YOUR BODY

You don't need me to tell you that the only person who can do anything about the physical state you're in is you. The only reason you are going to get in shape is because you want to, not because anybody else tells you that you must. If you are asked why you don't drop some weight and start working out, your reply is, 'Because I don't want to.' That should shut them up. Of course, you could be making excuses to yourself here, or it may be that you do want to lose weight because you suffer from low self-esteem/ no money/ no one to have sex with.

However, these are just passing thoughts. Don't rush in to exercising – start with a gentle warm-up, and while you are doing so, think of excuses not to change.

I CAN'T EXERCISE BECAUSE . . .

* I've got a weak back.
* My iron levels are unbalanced at the moment. (Only an expert will contradict you here, and it's a little-known fact that 'x' is an unknown quantity, and a 'spurt' is a drip under pressure.)
* I did myself a mischief in the health club jacuzzi.
* Someone else did me a mischief in the health club jacuzzi.
* The only exercise I enjoy is swimming, and the local pool is always brimming with snotty kids who wipe their noses on your costume and pee in the water.

* I'm not getting enough sex, and my lymph glands are sluggish.
* I look lousy in a lycra leotard.

The other thing about exercise is that it's useless in isolation. You have to give up all those

BAD HABITS

Oh no you don't. Excuses should be at your fingertips.

* Every time I give up smoking, I start drinking heavily again.
* Every time I give up drinking, I start smoking heavily again.
* So what – I only have dry vices.

✳   So what – I only have wet vices.

✳   Sho wot . . . (hic) I only have welsh rabbitsh . . . (hic).

✳   I haven't got a hangover, thanguverymuch ! It must be something I ate last night.

✳   I hadn't eaten, so the two glasses of white wine I had at dinner, which I also didn't eat, must have gone straight to my head.

✳   The wine must have been corked, I feel terrible.

✳   I'm under a lot of pressure at the moment – maybe getting drunk is the only way I can get you to notice that I'm not myself, that there's something wrong.

✳   So, I eat too much chocolate. Have you ever stopped to consider that it might not be entirely my fault, darling? After all, chocolate is a sex substitute, you know, it's all to do with pheromones, and God knows I'm not getting enough sex.

✳   I wasn't actually picking my nose. I was trying to trim my nose hairs, went in a bit far, and appear to have lost the nasal hair-trimming scissors up there somewhere . . . can you see where they went?

✳   I fell on my fingers.

✳   You may think that's what I was doing .. I couldn't possibly comment.

✳   Nose picking ? Not me. I may, or may not be a freemason in the process of communicating to another.

✳   You knew I was a total slob when you married me.

OK, so nose-picking doesn't have a great deal to do with whether or not you exercise, but a bad habit is a bad habit and you might as well have excuses for the lot of 'em.

LIFE AND YOUR ROLE IN IT – HOW NOT TO HAVE TO EXPLAIN THAT YOU HAVEN'T GOT ONE

Come on, how many people do you know who have a role in life? Most of us just muddle on through as best we can. But sometimes you find that Other People will try and impose some sort of role on you and it's as well to be prepared. It's no good getting on your high horse, demanding to know what right they have to judge or disapprove, asking whether they've ever heard of Equal Rights and Amnesty International? No, it's excuse time again.

There's not going to church:

* If there is a God, and He allows so many disasters to happen, I'm not sure I want to go round to his house.
* I'm in the process of reconsidering my beliefs.
* If there's a God up there, she will understand, as a woman, that I simply don't have the time to go to church.
* All that corruption and embezzlement of funds and priests who take vows of celibacy and then get their secretaries pregnant on the side – I can get all that at the office.
* Oh, come on, it's nothing to do with religion these days, is it? It's all Vatican Express, don't leave Rome without it, and did you know that the word 'Audit' doesn't appear anywhere in the Bible.
* Actually, I'm into a more progressive form of Christianity these days: similar rituals, half the guilt. We don't have wine and wafers, we have Jack Daniels and magic mushrooms. If you don't see Jesus then, you never will.

Not being green or politically correct. There is much pressure to be aware of these issues and to talk them up in the correct way. Try taking an opposing, unpopular view, just for the hell of it:

* The universe, and our oceans, are enormous places, and we're not going to pollute the whole flaming lot in our lifetime . . . well, why should I care what becomes of it all after I'm dead?

(You may or may not mean this, of course, but it'll cause such a stink that you'll be dining out on your challenger's reaction and subsequent arrest for ABH for months.) And there's more. . .

* Were you aware that the value of the contents of the average domestic dustbin is a mere 5p all-in?
* I'd spend more on petrol driving to the recycling point than I'd save by recycling the bottles and papers and cans. Plus I'd be polluting the environment at the same time.
* Actually I'm looking for a new recycling point. I had an unpleasant experience at the one up the road. . . no, I would not care to elaborate. . . would you happen to know of anywhere else?

BRUSHES WITH THE LAW

They happen to us all – parking offences and speeding are the most common – and they are golden opportunities to practise your excusatory skills:

❋   I'm making a delivery. See how I load and unload, Officer !

❋   The baby was throwing up. (If you have no baby, grab one from the nearest passing pram, or start fumbling in the wastepaper bin on the pavement beside your car – you were holding her over it a minute ago, 'she must be in here somewhere.')

❋   I suddenly spotted an armed robbery taking place at that bank across the street, at least I thought I did and I stopped here to find a phone box so that I could call the police.

❋   I got a call on my mobile and I know it's illegal to speak on a portable while you're driving, so I thought I'd just pull in here.

❋   My brakes failed . . . oh, look, they're all right now, that's amazing.

❋   I could suddenly smell gas, and I panicked.

❋   I was being followed. I think I've lost them though . . .

❋   I was trying to get home before I got drunk . . .

❋   I was trying to get home before I fell asleep . . .

❋   I thought it was a bit narrow for a motorway.

❋   Sprechen-sie Deutsch ?

Also see Case History 'I'm awfully sorry, Officer, but . . .' (page 30)

YOU AND YOUR CONSCIENCE

Why you haven't got a promotion, why you haven't got around to doing the decorating but manage to watch plenty of TV, why you haven't done any of the dynamic things you thought you were going to do when you were eighteen – you've got excuses for them all, I'm sure. So what can I tell you? You deceive yourself. Well that's not strictly true – in fact, you're the one who's best positioned to explain why things are as they are.

For example, any right-thinking mortal would be able to see that the reason you haven't got a promotion is that you've been too busy concentrating on doing up the house, and what a load of problems you've had with those blasted builders, don't they just pull the wall over your eyes, they want shooting . . . You haven't got around to doing the decorating? Well, of course not, you've been focusing all your energies on your job and pulling out the stops to land that promotion this year. Vegetate in front of the telly? Not me! If you took the trouble to look closer you would spot the foolscap pad and ballpoint on my lap. What I'm actually doing is mapping out my fabulously dynamic future. TV drama gives me a lot of ideas, you know. In fact, I was watching that radio DJ detective thing the other night, you know the one that always ends up with the guy saying 'Goodnight, America, wherever you are', and I thought, what absolutely diabolical dialogue, even I can do better than that. And as I sat there I started to scribble, tentatively at first, then boldly and with soaring confidence, and in fact I think I actually have what it takes to write TV drama myself, and so now I need to watch a lot of TV to get a good feel for what's out there right now and how I could improve it, and . . .

EXCUSES FOR ALL OCCASIONS

Well, not all occasions – this is the chapter where we cover all the bright ideas we had when we first planned the book that don't seem to fit in anywhere else.

WHY MY CHEQUE WASN'T IN THE POST

❋ It was. At least, I thought it was. They must have had another break-in at the post office/fire in the post box/someone emptying the baby's potty in there, you wouldn't believe the stuff these hooligans do/put into post boxes.

WHY I AM TWO HOURS LATE FOR DINNER

❋ A funny thing happened to me on my way here to dinner this evening. . .

At which point you divert attention from your tardiness by telling the latest screamingly hilarious joke. If you don't know any, start cultivating the friendship (and paying the bar bills) of someone who always seems to have heard the latest. Read the newspapers and gossip magazines avidly – these excuses work even better if you can tailor the joke to the latest government misdemeanour or royal faux pas.

Sorry I'm two hours late Susie.. Had I known it was going to be my mother I wouldn't have picked up the phone

If you master the art of joke-telling well enough, you will eventually find that you have a reputation for being everybody's perfect dinner guest and will be inundated with invitations to soirées both you and your hosts know you are going to be late for; indeed, this is part of the gag – it becomes your renowned party piece, and dinners will be scheduled around you, so that you have to learn even more jokes, and so it goes on, to the point that you start wondering whether you are a dinner guest or a court jester for Chrissakes. Don't get paranoid, though, it's not all bad: ultimately you may even have to consider a possible career change, getting an agent, and start wondering whether fame and fortune will change you (NB: sack the cleaning lady, now – see under The Ifs and Buts of Domestic Bliss, page 90).

Alternatively, a more serious approach: a glance at the evening paper may provide just the alibi you are seeking – that flash flood, crumbling office block, multiple pile-up, towering inferno was the thing that held you up. Everyone likes a hero.

WHY I DIDN'T INVITE YOU TO MY PARTY

✱ But I sent out your invitation ages ago! I thought it odd that you never replied . . . you'll probably get it during the next week or so (then hastily slip one in the post, remembering to back-date it).

✱ But you were there! We spoke! We drank! We danced . . . Oh, how we danced! We snogged, even . . . What do you mean, that wasn't you?

✱ I decided to have one party for my dull friends, and one for my more interesting friends. (This is clever, as you never actually conclude your explanation . . . only a real dummy would demand to know into which category she fell. You are off the hook.)

* The dog ate my Filofax, and I didn't have your number or address.
* But, sweetie, you're a vegetarian and it was a carnivores' party.

WHY I'M TRYING TO AVOID HAVING THAT DRINK WITH THE NEW NEIGHBOURS

* They don't look my type.
* He drives a BMW, for God's sake and he won't want to talk about my Reliant Robin.
* I'm too annoyed about the fence, and I don't trust myself to be tactful after a couple of Martinis. . . it's their bloody fence that side, you know . . .
* I understand that she used to be in fast food packaging, and my husband's an eco-terrorist. I don't trust him to be tactful after a couple of Martinis.
* You've got to be very careful getting too thick with neighbours too soon: It's a bit like being on a cruise; talk to anyone on the first day and you find yourself stuck with them for the entire fortnight.

AND FINALLY . . .

There comes a time to stop being squeamish , and this is it. But, if you are the type who blushes a vibrant red at the mere thought of coming up with a good excuse, it might help to put yourself in the noble boots of Napoleon Bonaparte. 'Not tonight, Josephine' must be the most celebrated pre-cuse in history. What excuse it was leading up to, we'll never know – but it would have to be on a par with 'Sorry, I'm washing my hair', 'The cheque's in the post', or 'I'll only put it in a little way'. Thinking about it, you've got to feel sorry for old Boney, haven't you? Imagine being remembered more for a three-word expression heaving with impotence than for any number of bloody imperial victories. Still, everybody meets their Waterloo.

Once you have embraced the idea of the excuse as the ultimate social parachute, the world's your oyster. Never again need you be caught with your pants down, or up, your hand in the till, asleep on the job, without an answer, decoy, diversion, accomplice, get-out clause or reason to be cheerful.

Good luck. What?. . . page 156? The one promising all the juicy bits?. . .No, sorry, I didn't get around to writing that. You know how it is, deadlines loom, deadlines pass, editors moan, and you begin to run out of excuses. That's my excuse and I'm sticking to it.